Really Useful Guides

Genesis 1–11

The Bible Reading Fellowship
15 The Chambers, Vineyard
Abingdon OX14 3FE
brf.org.uk

The Bible Reading Fellowship (BRF) is a Registered Charity (233280)

ISBN 978 0 85746 791 1
First published 2019
10 9 8 7 6 5 4 3 2 1 0
All rights reserved

Text © Rebecca S. Watson 2019
This edition © The Bible Reading Fellowship 2019
Cover illustration by Rebecca J Hall

The author asserts the moral right to be identified
as the author of this work

Acknowledgements

Scripture quotations are taken from The New Revised Standard Version of the Bible, Anglicised edition, copyright © 1989, 1995 by the Division of Christian Education of the National Council of the Churches of Christ in the United States of America. Used by permission. All rights reserved.

Every effort has been made to trace and contact copyright owners for material used in this resource. We apologise for any inadvertent omissions or errors, and would ask those concerned to contact us so that full acknowledgement can be made in the future.

A catalogue record for this book is available from the British Library

Printed and bound in the UK by Zenith Media NP4 0DQ

Really Useful Guides

Genesis 1–11

Rebecca S. Watson

Series editor: Simon P. Stocks

For James

Each Really Useful Guide focuses on a specific biblical book, making it come to life for the reader, enabling them to understand the message and to apply its truth to today's circumstances. Though not a commentary, it gives valuable insight into the book's message. Though not an introduction, it summarises the important aspects of the book to aid reading and application.

This Really Useful Guide to Genesis 1—11 will transform your understanding of the biblical text, and will help you to engage with the message in new ways today, giving confidence in the Bible and increasing faith in God.

Contents

1	Why read Genesis 1—11?	7
2	What is Genesis 1—11?	12
3	What does Genesis 1—11 say?	15
4	How does Genesis 1—11 say it?	17
5	Where do these stories come from?	21
6	Reading Genesis 1—11 today	30
7	Tips for reading Genesis 1—11 and what to look for	35
	Creation (1:1—2:4)	35
	The garden of Eden (2:4—3:24)	43
	Cain and Abel (4:1–16)	51
	The genealogies and associated stories (4:17—5:32, 9:28—10:32, 11:10–32)	56
	The sons of God and the daughters of men (6:1–4)	62
	The flood: sin, flood, sacrifice, blessing and covenant (6:5—9:17)	66
	Noah's drunkenness and the cursing of Ham (9:18–27)	81

	The Tower of Babel (11:1–9)	85
8	**Genesis 1—11 in the Bible**	92
9	**Questions for reflection or discussion**	94

1

Why read Genesis 1—11? A personal reflection

When I was a child, I was an avid reader of animal stories. *Tarka the Otter*, *Watership Down* and *Duncton Wood* inspired in me a passion for conservation and animal welfare. After immersing myself in James Herriot's books I was determined to become a vet – though after being given James Galway's autobiography, I harboured ambitions to become a flautist. These stories were incredibly powerful, and they did a great deal to shape my outlook on life, even if my veterinary and musical ambitions were in the end to be frustrated by lack of talent and by a focus on other interests.

The stories I enjoyed invited me momentarily to step into the shoes of someone else, so that when I turned the last page or walked out of the cinema, I saw the world a little bit differently. I came away with a changed sense of purpose or priority, or with a better understanding of others' situations. I was moved by the stories of the hidden lives of animals that conveyed their struggles and the threats posed by human activity in a way that statistics and non-fiction books never could. I was inspired by the dedication of James Galway, and later by *Billy Elliot* and the Olympians in *Chariots of Fire* (not that I was ever foolish enough to imagine I might become a dancer or runner myself). Anything on a romantic or family theme always leaves me with a renewed sense of the primary importance of love and relationships over everything else, and I'm probably a bit nicer for a little while afterwards as a result.

Stories inspire us to action, too. All letters from charities asking for our support engage us with the situation of a particular individual in need, compelling us to empathise with their predicament. The most memorable sermons usually have a story at their heart, which we might remember long after the core message of the sermon itself. Advertisers realise the power of stories, too. John Lewis' Christmas adverts have attracted particular interest not by shouting about products and prices, but by engaging viewers with a personal story about Christmas, usually with a message around what this festival is 'really' about.

The way stories engage the imagination and invite a response has always appealed to me. Some people like truth to be tied down and concrete, through philosophy and science, through verifiable historical facts and measurable statistics. But I love the way that each time you read a story, you may gain a different perspective on it and discover new insights. Nowhere can you do this more than in Genesis 1—11, which in my view contains some of the most profound religious literature ever written.

Every time I read Genesis 2—3 in particular, I pick up new aspects of the story. It is so simple, yet so rich in what it implies. Take, for example, the reaction of Adam when he's confronted by God after eating the fruit. He says, 'The woman whom you gave to be with me, she gave me fruit from the tree, and I ate' (3:12). In other words: 'Don't look at me, God. It's your fault, and hers.' I suspect that pretty well sums up my instinctive response when I have done something wrong: it's so easy to lay the blame elsewhere rather than accepting personal responsibility.

I also value the way Genesis 1—11 challenges me as a reader and provokes further questions and thought. I can't remember when I first read these chapters, and if you were raised in a Christian family or were taught Bible stories at school it may be the same for you. One of my most striking memories of Genesis, though, comes from watching my daughter engaging with the creation accounts. When she was quite young, she came out of Sunday school saying they'd been learning the order of the days of creation, but she was 'no good at it' because she'd misremembered the sequence. A week or two later, she was looking at a children's Bible and began to comment on what 'dominion' might (and should!) mean. She wanted to know what I thought about how the story might fit with what she knew of evolution and gender equality. She was asking questions of the stories and connecting them with her own knowledge, values and experience. I can't say I had all the answers, but Genesis was a brilliant prompt for a conversation that we wouldn't otherwise have had, and it made us both think more deeply about important questions.

It's easy to be stuck, with a story known from childhood, in just remembering and recognising its details and not thinking beyond them. Sadly, church doesn't always help us move beyond that. But simply taking these stories at a surface level rather misses the point. Deeper reading involves understanding, questioning and making connections with other aspects of experience. This is something that Genesis 1—11 positively invites, even if we don't always find clear-cut answers we can all agree on.

As you read each part of Genesis 1—11 for yourself, try to ask yourself what its message might be and how its perspectives on the world might fit with yours. What questions does it raise for you, and what insights can it offer? I hope you will find these chapters as inspiring as I have.

2

What is Genesis 1—11?

Genesis 1—11 is many things. Most importantly, it's a prologue to the rest of Genesis and to the Bible as a whole. To understand how it works, let's draw a comparison with the gospels. You might be aware that Mark's gospel dives straight into the story of Jesus' ministry. Matthew and Luke, however, wanted to provide a bit of the backstory to Jesus by speaking of his birth and childhood. In the process, they reveal important things about who he was and about what he was to do in his adult life: his mission to the poor, his kingship and death, the message of hope and joy at his birth and so on. John's gospel goes a stage further by beginning with creation itself, describing Jesus as the incarnate Word.

Genesis as a whole has a similar function to the prologues of Matthew, Luke and John. It provides the 'backstory' to the people of Israel. The story of Israel really begins with the exodus out of Egypt (and so with the book of Exodus), but the background to their origins is provided by Genesis 12—50, with the stories of Abraham and his family, their earliest ancestors. Just as Matthew and Luke offer insights into Jesus' adult life through relating stories of his early years, so the stories of Abraham, Isaac and Jacob already introduce key aspects of God's relationship with Israel: election, covenant, promise and so on. Genesis 1—11, however, is like the prologue in John's gospel. It goes right back to the beginning and shows that, from the first, God's commitment was to the whole world. Like John's gospel, it explores profound questions about God, but it does so through stories. It invites the reader to think, wonder and be challenged about these issues before the story of Israel has even begun.

Genesis 1—11 also serves to set the story of God's relationship with his people within the wider context of his relationship with all of humanity and indeed with creation itself. It makes clear that God is the originator of the whole world, and that when he looked at all that he had made, he saw it was very good. His commitment and interest, therefore, is focused on all of creation. The series of events outlined in Genesis 2—11 show how human sin became a barrier that repeatedly disrupted that relationship until finally God confused the languages of the peoples and scattered them over the face of the earth so that they could no longer scheme together. The election of Abraham in Genesis 12 is a response to this changed situation, but even then the intention is that through him all the families of the earth (not just Abraham's family) would be blessed. When we turn to the end of the Bible, we see a reversal of Babel in the speaking in 'tongues' at Pentecost, and the New Testament also witnesses to the hope that all tongues will confess Jesus as Lord and that creation itself will be renewed.

This means that although the Bible is mainly about the story of God's chosen people – Israel, Judah, Jesus, the disciples, the early church – God's story is much bigger, for his concern from first to last is with all creation.

3

What does Genesis 1—11 say?

You may be familiar with Rudyard Kipling's *Just So Stories* and similar traditional tales, such as 'how the leopard got his spots' or 'how the snake lost its legs'. These children's stories are a fun way of explaining why things are the way they are. In many ways, Genesis 1—11 performs a similar function.

The stories of Genesis 1—11 describe (among other things) how creation came about, how we fit somewhere in-between God and the animals, how paradise was lost, how human culture and technology developed and how different peoples and tribes descended from each other and from a common parent. They explain why childbirth and farming are so hard, why there are different nations and languages and ultimately how God ended up selecting one people out of all the different human groups on earth, even though he is God of all. Genesis 1—11 also has quite a lot to say about how sin arises and is dealt with. Oh, and along the way, it also explains how the snake lost its legs.

What exactly Genesis 1—11 says about all these topics is something we'll come on to when we look at the stories themselves. But first, let's think more about what sort of stories these are.

4

How does Genesis 1—11 say it?

The stories of Genesis 1—11 address some of the most important questions about life, existence and everything else that really matters: who are we? Where do we come from? What has gone wrong in the world and how can it be put right? These are questions that philosophers ask and discuss in abstract terms. But Genesis 1—11 addresses them through narrative that puts God at the centre.

Biblical scholars use a particular term to describe this kind of storytelling: 'myth'. Please don't be alarmed! You're probably thinking that when we talk about 'myths' in everyday speech, we usually mean 'something that isn't true'. This is really unfortunate, as the technical meaning is almost the exact opposite: these are stories concerned with the truth. They express truth about God and about the world told through story. These are stories that ask and answer deep questions, that talk of God and humanity, and that always have questions of meaning at their core. They may not always be about things that once happened in the measurable, historical sense, but they concern things that always happen: they are profoundly true.

When we see Adam and Eve tempted, longing for knowledge, but finding they instead have to face mortality and limitation, we know this applies to all of us. The basic insight that God is God of all creation and is responsible for everything that exists, that he was there right from the beginning and will be always, is not just a story confined to Genesis, but it underpins the whole of the rest of the Bible and our life of faith today.

One of the brilliant things about stories is that there is no limit to the number you can tell. Genesis 1—11 takes advantage of that and starts by relating two stories of creation. Both offer contrasting perspectives, but by putting them together the compilers of the book were able to offer a 'both-and' view of creation. The two creation stories have really important (and quite different) things to say, so they're both included.

By putting them together, Genesis 1—11 is able to show that God is the amazing, powerful, transcendent

God who gives order and structure to the cosmos (as in the first creation story, 1:1—2:4). But, it tells us, he is also personally involved in his creation, forming his creatures out of clay, breathing his own breath into them to animate them and engaging with individuals' lives (as in the second story, 2:4–25). Look out for the differences between the two stories as you read them. You might find one easier to relate to than the other, but, by having both, we are challenged to hold both pictures of God together.

It's a bit less noticeable, but it seems that two versions of the flood story are woven together too, with each expressing different perspectives on the same topic – but we'll come on to that later.

There are also lots of stories in Genesis 1—11 about human wrongdoing, known as sin. We're shown how, as human transgression escalates, it takes different forms and has varied consequences, and so we're invited to think quite broadly about this too.

This sharing of insights and perspectives tells us something else about how Genesis 1—11 speaks and how we should read it: it explores sometimes quite contrasting ideas about God, life and what it is to be human. Truth can't always be pinned down to a single proposition, but big questions need to be thought about from different angles and sometimes given more than one answer. Genesis 1—11 invites us to engage our imaginations and to think creatively.

5

Where do these stories come from?

Are there stories that you feel that you have 'always known', ever since you were young? Some stories have been told and retold so many times without being written down that it can be very difficult to trace their origins.

So it is with Genesis 1—11. We actually know quite a bit about what was happening in Israel and Judah and the world around in biblical times. The difficulty is in knowing how the stories of Genesis 1—11 fit within this picture, not least because parts of these chapters may have come into being at different times. The stories we have in our Bibles now might have been told long before they were first written down, and they may have been changed as they were passed on by word of mouth.

One thing we do know is that there were accounts of creation and of a flood that were told long before the

Bible came into being. Many details are very similar to the story of Noah. We have narratives from ancient Assyria and Babylonia (modern Iraq) which not only tell of a flood but describe how the flood hero, known as either Atrahasis or Utnapishtim, is instructed to build a boat of wood, reed and pitch, which he then fills with animals. After the flood comes for seven days and nights, he lands on a mountain and sends out birds to see if the waters have abated, before offering a sacrifice once they safely reach dry land. So it is clear that stories of creation and flood in their earliest written form precede the Bible by many centuries.

It has even been suggested that there is geological evidence for a massive flood when the Bosporus, which joins the Mediterranean and Black Seas, was dramatically breached about 7,000 years ago. Possibly this event might have prompted stories (and explanations) which were passed on over thousands of years.

Probably the authors of the Bible knew of such tales, since traders passed through Israel-Palestine on their way between Egypt and Mesopotamia or when bringing goods to and from the Mediterranean. Much of the influence behind the Old Testament comes from the time of the exile, when some of the inhabitants of Judah were forcibly removed from their homeland and taken elsewhere in the Babylonian empire. Here, they were more directly exposed to stories and beliefs local to where they settled. For example, we know that in Babylon, there was a New Year festival, at which their story of creation was told. Possibly, awareness of these early creation and flood accounts (and the need to tell a counter story) particularly stemmed from this time.

However, this background is only part of the evidence, because the biblical accounts are very distinctive. They don't just differ in detail from the Babylonian flood story, for example in naming the flood hero Noah, but they seek to tell a different story altogether because they have their own particular understanding of God. Remember, these are not just stories for the sake of it, nor are they merely traditions of 'what happened'. The most important thing is that they're told to convey particular ideas about God, humanity and the rest of creation. In fact, probably one of the main reasons for including these stories in the Bible is to retell them in a way that shows the God of Israel to be the only God. In the Babylonian versions of the flood story, one god wanted to destroy humanity and another one rescued the chosen survivors. The idea that one God did both must have seemed revolutionary, but it's the only way of telling it if this God is the only God and there are no others.

The first creation story also seems to go out of its way to counter beliefs in more than one god (known as polytheism). For example, it doesn't talk about the creation of the sun and moon but of the greater and lesser lights. This is probably because the word for 'sun' was also the name of the sun god, and that for 'moon' was likewise also the name of the moon god. Now they are demoted to 'lights', given the task of ruling the day and night by the God who made them.

So Genesis 1—11 tells the stories of creation and the flood deliberately and self-consciously to espouse faith in the God of the Old Testament, rather than in other deities. This could have occurred in a wide range of contexts, but the time of the exile in about 586BC, when many were uprooted from their homes and faced with foreign religious practices, or some time afterwards, may offer the best fit. In that period, the temptation must have been very great to follow the apparently powerful and triumphant god of Babylon, Marduk, after the destruction of Jerusalem and the capture of its king and leading citizens. You might also have noticed that the tower that was built up to heaven in Genesis 11 is the 'Tower of Babel', which is another name for Babylon. This also suggests a particular concern with the overweening pride of the dominant power of that time.

The exile would also have presented challenges to what must previously have been quite a localised faith. It would have raised the question of whether God could be worshipped and active away from his land. Many people would have been tempted to think that he had been defeated by the more powerful gods of Babylon. In the end, though, the authors of the Bible concluded that God wasn't only a local, tribal god, but the God of all creation. Nowhere was outside of his rule and concern. The fall of Jerusalem and deportation of its leaders had not happened because he was weak but because he was Lord of all the earth and active in the affairs of other nations. He was able to use Babylon as a means of punishing his people and bringing them back to him because he was the only God (or, at least, considerably more powerful than the gods of the Babylonians).

Another important aspect of biblical thought at this time was the belief that the failure of the kingdoms of Israel and Judah was due to the people's sin and turning away from God. Possibly, then, this preoccupation is reflected in the cycle of sin and punishment that runs throughout Genesis 1—11, ending with the dispersal of humanity across the earth.

One of the most challenging aspects of the fall of Jerusalem was the end of the monarchy. However, one consequence of this was a renewed emphasis on God's kingship and a transfer of some aspects of kingship on to God's people as a whole. This tendency can be seen in the creation stories too. The idea that all humanity, male and female, is made in the image of God is so familiar to us that it is easy to overlook how revolutionary it probably was. It was commonplace for kings in the ancient Near East to claim that they were the sons of gods and made in their image. We even have a hint of this in the Old Testament. Have a look at Psalm 2:7, where God seems to describe the king as 'my son'. For Genesis to extend this to all of humanity is therefore very striking. It has huge implications for the value put on each human being and is a motivation behind all sorts of Christian humanitarian action, but already in the Old Testament it goes hand in hand with laws in which people are treated equally, whether they are a king or commoner. This is very different from the ideas held in much of the ancient world, for example in Hammurabi's law codes. In the Old Testament the same punishments are applicable to all (though unfortunately slaves are, perhaps inevitably, seen primarily as property, and women often are too).

Of course, it would be foolish to think that all the stories in Genesis 1—11 originated at the same time, or that they haven't undergone some development to reach the form with which we're familiar today. It's perhaps not surprising, then, to find that some parts of this collection show traces of interest in the temple. This is particularly the case (though not very obviously so) in connection with the garden of Eden story. Eden is mentioned elsewhere in the Old Testament, in the book of Ezekiel, where it is described as 'the garden of God' and 'the holy mountain of God' (Ezekiel 28:13–14). Gardens were particularly associated with royal palaces, but here Eden is implicitly connected with God's palace, the temple. (The words for 'palace' and 'temple' are the same in Hebrew.) In fact, there are lots of reasons to see Eden as modelled on the temple. For example, the Jerusalem temple had a huge container of water, the 'cast sea' (1 Kings 7:23–26), and the idealised pictures of the future temple in Ezekiel 47 and Revelation 21 envisage a river flowing out from it to nourish the earth, just as the river flows out of Eden (Genesis 2:10). Adam's task in the garden was 'to till it and keep it' (Genesis 2:15), and these are the same verbs usually used of temple service, where priests and Levites would 'serve and guard' the tabernacle (Numbers 18:4), just as the people should 'serve' God and 'keep' his commandments (Deuteronomy 10:12–13). The fruitfulness of the garden is echoed in the temple decoration, which was adorned with foliage and plants. The branched menorah (lampstand), which is still an important symbol in Judaism, is thought to be a stylised tree. Even the guardian cherubim belong as much in the temple as at the gates of Eden, since the Lord is often described as enthroned upon the cherubim which were on the ark of the covenant (Exodus 25:17–22; Numbers 7:89), and the curtains of the tabernacle were adorned with cherubim (Exodus 26:1).

The difficulty comes in trying to connect these ideas with any specific historical context, since they will undoubtedly have been very ancient and have endured for a long time. Some people think that this particular focus should be associated with the first temple in Jerusalem during the time of the early monarchy. Do you agree? It's really very hard to be sure either way. Instead of linking the story with the establishment of these important institutions, we could equally think it belongs in the time after their loss, when ideas associated with the priesthood or king may have been applied to the people as a whole. Once the physical temple in Jerusalem was no longer present, the idea of an ideal garden of God, modelled on the temple but existing irrespective of it, might have become more important. In this respect, we might remember that the idea of the river flowing out from the temple or heavenly city in Ezekiel and Revelation belongs to visions of an ideal future, not to a concrete place. Their hope for a new temple and a closer relationship with God comes from a time of suffering after the temple itself (the first one in Ezekiel's case, and the second in Revelation's) had been destroyed.

6

Reading Genesis 1—11 today

One of my favourite books is a children's picture book called *When the World Was New* by Alicia Garcia de Lynam. It offers an imaginative retelling of how God may have gone about creation, from when he sews stars on to a big cloth sky, cuts out paper chains of people and knits sheep to when he finally pulls the light cord next to his fluffy cloud to turn off the light before going to sleep after his work.

Now, I do not really think that God literally created the world this way any more than I believe that Shreddies are 'knitted by Nanas', despite what the adverts tell us. But the fantastic thing about this book is that it invites us to think of creation in fresh ways and, from this, to conjure up all sorts of other possibilities and improbabilities without having to settle on any one picture. It invites us to wonder, and indeed to relish not knowing, how it happened. It helps us to realise that we do not fully understand the ways of God rather than leading us into the illusion of thinking we know more than we do.

I think the stories of Genesis 1—11 are more like this than we realise. They don't generally offer very specific images of how God made certain things – we are left to fill in those gaps in our own imagination. However, they do invite us to think about different possibilities rather than confining ourselves to one version. To take one obvious example, we're presented with two creation accounts, not one. They are so very different that they invite us to think about God, ourselves and the rest of creation through different lenses and to realise that we can accept alternatives rather than pinning ourselves down too much.

Similarly, two versions of the flood story seem to be woven together, allowing us to absorb their different perspectives and perhaps to imagine more. Did you know that the idea that 'the animals came in two by two' belongs to one version, but the other has the more complex idea that there were seven pairs of every clean animal and one pair of each unclean one? Have a look at Genesis 6:19–20 and 7:8–9 and then compare 7:2–3. Our popular culture has latched on to the idea of there being two of each animal more easily, but giving toy Noah's arks to children so that they can invent their own stories and retell the old one with their own elaborations is in keeping with the spirit of this writing. These stories, set long, long ago and far, far away in Babylon and Ararat and Eden are to be enjoyed, thought about, imagined and retold.

The stories of Genesis 1—11 invite reflection but also wonder. What does it mean to be human? How do we relate to other animals, God and each other? How do we understand the paradox of human potential and limitation, and how should we respond to this? Can we ever sustain a relationship with God or each other without sin getting in the way? When you read Genesis 1—11, familiarity with the stories might limit your imagination. But if you can free yourself from focusing on the detail of what happened when, you will hopefully be able to reflect on the deeper issues with which the stories are really concerned. You might even like to think of your own answers to these big questions before reading Genesis and then see how the Bible's view compares with and might enrich or challenge your own.

We also need to note that Genesis 1—11 is a sequential narrative. The story of Adam and Eve leads into that of Cain and Abel, and so on as the generations progress. But this is not just a story of 'progress'.

Although these chapters depict the development of human culture – the building of cities, the planting of vineyards and so on – we also see repeated instances of transgression.

This is why it is important not just to read Genesis 3 on its own. It is part of a bigger picture, as the first of a series of stories of sin and punishment. Humanity did not just disobey God's command in the garden of Eden. Rather, this was one of many such events, some of them told here in Genesis and others further into the Bible. Each of them required action by God to punish wrongdoing and to prevent further recurrence. But in each case there is also some mitigation, suggesting continued commitment and care on God's part even where punishment and prevention are inevitable. The first human couple are cast out of the garden, but given clothes to cover themselves; Cain is also excluded, but marked to ensure his protection; the flood washes away the polluted earth, yet provision is made to enable some to survive; the peoples are dispersed and their languages are confused, yet God chooses one man, Abram, through whom all will ultimately be blessed.

When seeking to understand Genesis 1—11, it is important therefore to remember to look for the themes and messages in this continuous narrative, rather than just interpreting sections on their own. As you read each of the stories of sin, pay attention to what the transgression is, what God says and how he responds, but also what action he takes to limit the damage and to ensure the continuation of humanity and of his relationship with them.

As you read Genesis 1—11, see if you can spot the concerns of the original writers. What message were they trying to convey? Then think about how its themes translate into our own context. For example, the human urge to transcend our natural limits – to seek knowledge and immortality, to build up into the heavens and to become like God – is characteristic of the modern world. What do you think about genetic modifications, cloning or frozen embryos? Perhaps the ideas of Genesis 1—11 will aid your reflections. Questions about the relation between the sexes and about humanity's proper place relative to other creatures are no less topical. Genesis does not offer clear-cut answers – or if it does, their interpretation is debated enough for uncertainty to remain. However, it does raise questions that should be at the forefront of our agenda and it provides plenty of food for thought.

7

Tips for reading Genesis 1—11 and what to look for

Genesis 1—11 begins with two of the best-known (and most interesting) stories in the Bible: creation and the garden of Eden. These are followed by more classics: Cain and Abel, the flood and the Tower of Babel, besides a few other smaller and less well-known narratives. They're intended to be read in sequence, so that is what we'll do here, except for the genealogies, which are discussed together for convenience.

Creation (1:1—2:4)

Science tells us that conditions in the universe are perfectly 'tuned' to enable life. If the laws of nature were fractionally different, life would have been impossible. For example, if after the Big Bang the universe had expanded even minutely slower than it actually did, it would have collapsed back in on itself; on the other hand, if it had expanded with fractionally greater force, the planets and stars would have been unable to form. There are many other potential variables which, had they been only slightly different, would have precluded the conditions that enable life.

Genesis 1 comes from a completely different world from modern science, yet it too describes the establishment of initial conditions that would enable life not just to exist but to flourish. If you read up to verse 19, what stands out for you? The first four days of creation concern the founding of the basic structure of an ordered world. The passage depicts God as separating the waters above and below the earth – the ones providing rain and those feeding the rivers from beneath – so that the earth could emerge. The waters of the sea are gathered together to enable dry land to appear, and the alternation of day and night is another form of separation. The sun and moon then allow the regulation of times and seasons into days and years. It is a highly ordered environment, ready for life.

However, God also works in partnership with his creation to bring forth living things. Look back at the second part of day three (the beginning of plant life) and then read the verses concerning days five and six. What strikes you about how creation happens here? Do you notice how the earth itself brings forth the vegetation on day three and all kinds of creatures on day six, while the seas bring forth aquatic animals on day five? The birds which appear on the fifth day and the humans which are created on day six may well have been envisaged as being brought forth in the same way. After all, the idea that humanity came from the ground is a dominant theme in the second creation story. We see, too, that the sun and moon are tasked with regulating day and night and the passage of time, while the animals are blessed so that they can go forth and multiply. (Strictly speaking, this is gifted to the fish and humanity, but we should assume that the birds and land animals who are created in-between are also blessed with procreative capacities.) The earth is a vibrant, good and wonderful world, made for all kinds of life to flourish in abundance, with each having its place and generative potential. This is envisaged as part of God's ongoing purpose for creation.

If you've ever constructed something in separate parts and then assembled them to make the final piece, you will be able to relate to God's evaluation of creation. Whether you're completing a Lego set, knitting the parts of a garment or engaging in a DIY project, it's only when all the pieces are put together that you appreciate how the whole is much more than the parts alone. Each day's work was 'good', but it is only when creation is complete that its 'very goodness' is evident. This might also prompt us to work for the conservation of the earth, since every extinction is a loss from that 'very good' whole created by God.

Verses 26–28 have attracted much debate, and you can see why they are perceived as so important. This is where we read that humanity is made in God's image. What do you think this might mean in the context of this creation story? There are lots of different views on what this means, though it seems to suggest a unique relationship with God and a distinctive role in relation to the rest of creation.

The idea that humanity is made in the divine image is repeated in 5:1–2, despite not appearing again in the rest of the Old Testament (though Psalm 8, with the idea that we are 'a little lower than God', implies a similar exalted status). In chapter 5 it is said that 'when God created humankind, he made them in the likeness of God'. We're then told that 'Adam… became the father of a son in his likeness, according to his image' (5:3). This suggests that being made in the image of God was passed down from one generation to the next. It could also mean that the sense in which human beings are made in the image of God is comparable with the way in which an individual may be the 'image' of their parent. This is not necessarily confined to physical appearance. After all, people can take after their parents in many ways and this was particularly so in the ancient world, where sons would usually work the same land or learn the same trade. It's also important to recall that the Old Testament does not think of body and mind or spirit as separate, but as part of the same indivisible person, so being made in someone's image may have been thought of in a more holistic way than is typical now.

However, there are other ways in which we can understand the idea of an 'image'. In the Old Testament, idols are also referred to as 'images' (e.g. Ezekiel 7:20; Amos 5:26) and were probably thought of as representing the presence of the god. When people tended the idol, they thought of themselves as in some sense ministering to the god it signified, and similarly if they prayed to it they understood themselves to be praying to the god through its image. So we might think of humans as in some sense representing God on earth. Have you noticed how modern autocratic rulers sometimes set up images of themselves to provide a constant reminder of their presence and control over the country? Kings in the ancient world did a similar thing, to communicate the reality of their reign in places where they might not be seen in person. Do you think human beings might be intended to mediate the presence or rule of God on earth?

If this idea is correct, it has important implications for how we should relate to other life on earth. Genesis clearly indicates that God values all of creation and intends it to flourish. At the same time, the idea that we should 'have dominion' over other creatures and 'subjugate' the earth sounds excessively harsh. Some people have assumed from this that the earth is here for us to exploit with impunity, but this seems wholly incompatible with the thought that human beings were made in the image of God and that other creatures are blessed by God too. Rather, we should probably understand the idea of 'dominion' and 'subjugation' in the way that we might talk of 'conquering' Everest. 'Conquering' in this sense means surviving an immense challenge, not having any appreciable impact on the mountain at all.

In fact, it can be helpful to read the three blessings of being fruitful and multiplying and filling the earth, subduing the earth and having dominion over other species as the direct opposite of the curses of chapter 3. Look at the blessings in 1:28 together with the curses in 3:15–19. Can you see any overlap in their concerns? There, in chapter 3, Eve will suffer pain in childbearing, but here, in chapter 1, fruitfulness is simply a blessed gift. There, humanity will struggle to bring forth food from the soil, but here there is the promise of subduing the earth. There, Eve and her offspring will suffer enmity with the serpent, a representative of the dangerous wild animals which threatened the lives of the ancient inhabitants of Palestine. Here, humans are invited instead to enjoy dominion over them. Through these blessings and the curses, we can understand something of the struggle to exist that has characterised the lives of most people ever since we appeared on the earth. The intention, then, seems to be that people should flourish, even though chapter 3 reflects the harsher reality of ongoing suffering in the face of hunger, predation and problems in childbirth.

Many readers talk of our relation to other creatures in terms of 'stewardship' – looking after the earth on behalf of God. This word does not appear in Genesis and some people are troubled by the idea of human domination that it might imply. However, if Christians understand being made in the image of God to mean that they should seek to relate to the earth and other creatures as they believe God himself would intend, then overall this must be a good thing.

Of course, the story of creation does not end here. There are two further institutions that need to be considered first. One is the provision of plants for food. The passage's silence on meat eating might simply reflect a customary diet in which meat was not often consumed: animals were not part of the writer's daily fare. However, it may derive from a sense that in an ideal world, and according to God's original intention, there would be no predation. If so, it matches the hope that there will be a future peaceable kingdom in which:

The wolf shall live with the lamb,
  the leopard shall lie down with the kid,
the calf and the lion and the fatling together,
  and a little child shall lead them.
ISAIAH 11:6

Another notable aspect of this creation account is that the institution of the sabbath starts here, at the very beginning. This makes an important point, that rest is woven into the fabric of creation and is part of the rhythm of life. But it is also a holy day, consecrated by God. If you look at the fourth of the ten commandments in Exodus 20, the command to keep the sabbath, it refers back to creation, since God 'rested on the seventh day; therefore the Lord blessed the sabbath day and consecrated it' (v. 11). This also explains the idea that rest applies equally to everyone: it is not just a human invention and a luxury for the wealthy, but built into creation, so it is natural that children, slaves and even livestock and resident aliens are included. Note also that God rested on the seventh day, inviting the thought that perpetual busyness is not a good model for life, nor the sign of status we might think. Now have a look back through the story and see if there are any other connections you might draw with contemporary life.

The garden of Eden (2:4—3:24)

I was recently given an anthology of poetry about the sea. One of the most striking things about it is its diversity. Some poets convey the terror of being caught out on the ocean in a storm, the destructiveness of waves pounding the coast, the tragic loss of life that it can cause. Others conjure up the beauty of sparkling waters, the soothing rhythm of gently breaking waves, the joy of summer holidays and childhood explorations into rock pools. A further group think more of the ships that travel across the ocean – elegant sailing boats, 'dirty British coasters', explorers' vessels, trawlers and warships. Of course, all of these poems conjure up something true about the sea, but by having such contrasting perspectives set side by side, it encourages the reader to take a broader view than any single poem would allow.

In many ways, having two creation stories in Genesis does the same thing. God in chapter 1 is the majestic, transcendent God, apparently standing outside and above creation, able to command things into being and to operate on a cosmic scale. But in the second creation account, in chapter 2, he is immanent: he's present and active on the earth, forming the human from the dust of the ground and watering the garden himself. By having the two stories side by side, we are invited to see God as *both* transcendent and immanent in creation, both superlatively powerful and intimately involved with his creation. Another way of looking at the difference between the two is to say that Genesis 1:1—2:4 is a creation story, but Genesis 2:4–25 is a story of origins. The second account presupposes the existence of the earth but is concerned more with how it was populated and in particular with the origins of humanity.

The story of the garden of Eden is one of the most familiar in the Bible, and is represented in art and advertising more than any other. I have to confess it's one of my favourite parts of the Old Testament, since its rich narrative invites rereading. Each time I return to it, different details strike me and offer new insights or raise fresh questions. You might like to think about what stands out for you in this story. What questions does it raise and what insights does it offer for you?

The trouble with a well-known story, though, is that sometimes what we think we know about it can diverge a bit from what it actually says. For example, it might be surprising to see that although the forbidden fruit is nearly always represented as an apple, the story itself doesn't actually say what it was. We also tend to think of the serpent as Satan. Given that in Revelation, Satan is described as 'that ancient serpent', it is not an unreasonable thing for later writers to have read back into Genesis, but we would be wrong to assume that this was the original intention, since 'Satan' only started to be seen as the author of evil in a much later period than Genesis was written.

Sometimes confusion or misunderstanding can arise when ideas are translated from one language or culture to another. This can happen with the description of Eve as her husband's 'helper' (2:18, 20), since for many modern readers it conjures up the idea of her as an assistant and her husband as the leader. However, this is not at all the case, since someone who is a 'helper' is often seen as the more powerful person, who protects or delivers the one who is helped (for example, in Joshua 1:14, where armed warriors 'help' wives and children), and God himself is described as a 'helper' or as helping in many cases. (For a few examples, see Genesis 49:25; 1 Samuel 7:12; Isaiah 41:10, 13–14; Psalm 54:4.) If anything, then, the word seems to reverse conventional gender roles rather than reinforcing them: the man needs his wife to help him, and without her he may find himself vulnerable or in distress. This is not to say she doesn't need him too: they will 'cling' or 'hold fast' to each other in marriage, stronger in mutual support than on their own.

Another detail that isn't obvious from many English translations is that *'adam* is the Hebrew word for 'human being', not a 'man' in the sense of being male. The word for a (male) man is only used in 2:23–24, directly after the creation of Eve, where the focus is on the relationship between the two of them. 'Adam' is not used as a personal name until 4:25, which describes how he became the father of Seth. This is really important, because 'Adam' is not at this point a named individual from a long time ago, but 'the human being'. In a way, then, he is Everyman. What we see of his disobedience and limitations, his struggles and hopes, applies to us all.

One feature of this story that stands out is the importance of the ground/soil. The term for this in Hebrew is *'adamah*, a word that is so close to *'adam* (human) that the writers play on the similarity to show how the human is an 'earth creature' which came from the soil, works it in life and returns to it in death. Some translators have even tried to reflect this in English, for example, by taking about 'humans' coming from the 'humus'. The idea that humans come from the ground is a valuable counterbalance to the motif of the 'image of God' that we see in Genesis 1. It's not that they cancel each other out. Rather, both contain aspects of the truth. Humans are part of the 'earth' community of living things, bound to the soil and, as mortals, will return to it. But they also have responsibilities towards other creatures and should reflect God's image on earth, even if they often fall a long way short of this calling.

In another wordplay, the serpent is described as 'clever, cunning' (*'arum*), whereas the humans are 'naked' (*'erom*) after realising their guilt. This rather reverses the assumption that human superiority applies all the time – though, on the other hand, awareness of nakedness is something that only seems to trouble our species, suggesting that guilt itself is a particularly human quality.

A further insightful characteristic of the story is its understanding of sin and temptation. Do you notice how the serpent cunningly sows seeds of doubt, implying that God is lying and keeping something for himself? The serpent makes eating the fruit sound justified, insinuating that it is the rule-setter, God, who is in the wrong, and he also dismisses the threat of negative consequences. Do you relate to Eve's response? She saw that the fruit was visually appealing, good to eat and held the promise of wisdom: she desired it, and so took it and also gave it to her husband. Then 'the human', instead of accepting responsibility for his own actions, blames everyone else, in this case the woman and even God. Aware of their sin, the couple then hide from God and suffer awareness of their own nakedness: they experience guilt and the fear of being exposed.

We see from the curses that all three miscreants suffer lasting consequences from their wrongdoing – and their shared crime also disrupts the previously harmonious relationship between them, with enmity lasting between the serpent's and woman's descendants.

One might imagine that 'the human's' blaming of his wife did nothing to foster good relations between them. It has been suggested that the curse on the woman that 'your desire shall be for your husband and he shall rule over you' (3:16) reflects a disrupted relationship, with the woman seeking to regain their previous unity and the man exploiting this. In any case, that suffering follows sin and has ongoing consequences is a clear outcome of this story.

Of course, the serpent is not the only one ever to have questioned why God prohibited the eating of this fruit, but this 'cunning' creature seems at least to state a half-truth. The fruit came from the 'tree of the knowledge of good and evil'. Have you ever wondered what this might be? At first glance, we might think that God, rather oddly, wanted to withhold moral wisdom from humans, as if he intended them not to know the difference between right and wrong. However, this sounds rather strange. In fact, 'knowledge of good and evil' seems to refer to special wisdom, since in 1 Kings 3:9, Solomon prays for an 'understanding mind to govern your people, able to discern between good and evil'. More importantly, God's words before he casts the couple out of the Garden correlate quite closely with what the serpent had already claimed:

See, the man has become like one of us, knowing good and evil; and now, he might reach out his hand and take also from the tree of life, and eat, and live forever.
GENESIS 3:22

In other words, 'knowing good and evil' is a divine quality which it is not appropriate for humans to have, any more than they should be immortal. The reality of human existence is that we are aware of mortality and long to resist it, but are subject to death; we long for wisdom, but cannot understand as much as we wish; we have moral discernment but fall short of our ideals; we aspire to greatness but often fail. This is the paradox and tragedy of being human: we are made in the image of God, but are far from being God, and are creatures of the dust who live with the pain of knowing that we will return there at the end of our lives. Of course, when this story is read together with the New Testament, in which Jesus is the new Adam, offering the promise of victory over sin and death (see 1 Corinthians 15:22), then there is the offer of a different ending to the story. However, being aware of earthly mortality and failure is still a defining aspect of the human condition.

Even read on its own, the story does not just end with punishment. After issuing the curses, God 'made garments of skins for the [hu]man and for his wife, and clothed them' (3:21). Once they are cast out of the garden, we also hear how Eve 'produced a man with the help of the Lord' (4:1). The blessing of giving forth new life remained with them. This pattern of continued divine care, even after people have been punished by God, runs through Genesis 1—11, as we shall see.

Cain and Abel (4:1–16)

Sadly, despite God's help in the begetting of Cain, the story does not continue well, with another account of sin and punishment following close on the last. If the temptation and guilt of chapter 3 sounds familiar from our own experience, the theme of sibling rivalry will no doubt resonate too, even if it does not usually end in murder.

We're not told why God accepted one offering and not the other, or even how this was evident. It has been suggested that the tale reflects a preference for a traditional pastoral way of life, rather than for the more 'modern', settled existence of the crop farmer. Many readers suppose that one sacrifice was unsatisfactory in some way or had been offered in the wrong spirit. Certainly, we are told that God 'had no regard' not just for Cain's offering but for Cain either (4:5). God's question to Cain after his angry response at rejection also suggests that Cain had been at fault: 'If you do well, will you not be accepted?' (4:7). However, instead of learning of the fault that had led to the rejection of his sacrifice, the story goes on to describe how in fury he plotted the murder of his brother, then sought to deny any knowledge of it.

One of the striking features of this story is how it connects with the previous one. Can you spot any keywords running between the two? In chapters 2—3, we learnt how the human came from the ground, but, after his disobedience, it was cursed because of him. The idea may well be that somehow the sin itself hurt the ground from which he had come and prevented it from flourishing and yielding food as before. The bond between *'adam* and *'adamah* had been injured. In chapter 4, Abel's blood cries out from the ground, since it had opened its mouth to receive his blood from Cain's hand. Interestingly, it is not the ground that is cursed this time, but Cain is 'cursed from the ground', which will no longer yield to him its strength. The curse against Cain has come from the ground, almost literally arising out of his sin. As a result he will 'be driven away from the soil [ground]' (4:14) and shall be hidden from the Lord's face, going 'away from the presence of the Lord' (4:16). The rupture of his ties to the soil goes hand in hand with alienation from God. Do you notice, too, how Cain had drawn his brother 'out into the field,' perhaps with the intention of his crime going unobserved? This story insists that nothing is hidden from God and that such a crime will have an impact on the earth, irrespective of human judicial procedures. The blood 'crying out' from the ground, like the Israelites 'crying out' from their slavery in Egypt, is a cry for justice and for God to respond.

A more surprising link with chapter 3 is the idea that sin's 'desire is for you, but you must master [rule over] it' (4:7). If you look carefully, you will see that same language is used in the curse of the woman, in which she is told that her desire will be for her husband but he will rule over/master her. Read together with chapter 4, it could fit with the notion that the woman is a temptress, performing the role of personified sin. There are reasons, though, to think that this is not the proper interpretation of the woman's role. For a start, she was intended as a helper to her husband, and one would hope that this should at least partially remain.

We should also expect the curse of the woman as something from which she would suffer more than the man. So, if one them is to be understood as harming the other here, it must be that the man's domination of her is the problem, rather than it being the righteous suppression of her sinful inclinations. In fact, a negative view of women as inclined to tempt men is not particularly characteristic of the Bible, though it is replete with colourful and flawed characters of both genders. The book of Proverbs does give a graphic description of Woman Folly, who sets out to entrap the young man to whom this section of its teachings is addressed, but she is set alongside her opposite, Woman Wisdom, who is a model of virtue and so is of priceless value to her husband. This suggests that overall the idea of women as temptresses does not hold.

Another aspect of the story that echoes the preceding one is God's kindness despite the punishment. Here, although Cain is cast out, he is given a mark that ensures his protection despite his vulnerability away from the presence of God.

Finally, something for you to think about that has always puzzled readers of this story: although it is set 'in the beginning', can you spot anything that might be incompatible with this context? Perhaps the most striking question is: who might kill Cain if he and his parents were the only people on earth? And why does he take Abel out into 'the field' to murder him, except to avoid being seen? A related issue arises in verse 17, since it mentions Cain's wife. Who was she? You might also notice that Abel was a keeper of sheep, even though Genesis 1 seems to invite a vegetarian diet. They could just have been kept for milk and wool or for sacrifice, of course, but seeing them mentioned here begs the question.

These logical anomalies might indicate that the story was not originally placed here, but eventually gravitated to its present position because its themes of sin and punishment, curse and the ground, fit so well. In fact, it may have begun as a story about the origin of the Kenites, a nomadic tribe (mentioned, for example, in Judges 1:16; 5:24) whose name could equally well be spelt 'Cainites'. Still, the fact that it could be placed after the story of the garden of Eden (and before the flood, when Cain's descendants would, in theory, have been wiped out) suggests that the compilers of Genesis did not understand the first chapters of this book in a strictly literal way. The archetypal function of the characters, and the emphasis on themes such as blessing and curse, sin and punishment, inform the narrative sequencing. It's a mistake to expect everything to fit together in a strictly literal way. Rather, these stories hold deeper truths about God, humanity and life on earth. As you look back through the story, ask yourself what you think its main purpose is.

The genealogies and associated stories (4:17—5:32, 9:28—10:32, 11:10–32)

Have you ever tried to trace your own family tree? Maybe you have even tried genetic profiling to find out if your ethnic mix is as you expect. The wish to discover more about one's origins can be quite compelling. People who have not known their birth parents often feel a desperate need to trace them. Even if there is no hope of locating living relatives, there is often a strongly held feeling that you need to know who your parents and grandparents were and where you came from in order truly to know who you are. Of course, anyone who delves deeply enough into their family tree is likely to discover ancestors of whom they can be proud, who achieved something notable in their lives, and other 'skeletons in the cupboard' revealing the hidden stories of the family members who may have done something that was viewed with shame.

Even a quick glance at our chapters reveals that genealogies are regarded as important by the compilers of Genesis 1—11. Hearing about someone else's family tree can be much less exciting than delving into one's own, and it can be tempting to feel the same way about the biblical genealogies. However, the point of these chains of 'begettings' is that this family tree is part of our shared story, remote as it may seem. It's worth remembering, too, that Luke's gospel takes pains to trace Jesus' own ancestry right back to 'Adam, son of God' (Luke 3:38), illustrating the Messiah's common bond with all humanity and perhaps (given the reference to God) with all God's creatures too.

It's the human details of family trees that brings them alive. Knowing someone's profession or snippets of their life story helps give a sense of a person in a way that a name on its own cannot. In the genealogies of Genesis 1—11, such details collectively build up a picture of the development of culture, escalating violence and the spread of humanity across the known world. Short asides identify the individuals who initiated cultural and technical developments, particularly in 4:20–22. We learn of when people began to 'invoke the name of the Lord' (4:26), while in 10:8, we hear of the first mighty warrior, Nimrod. As he is described as 'a mighty hunter before the Lord', it seems that he was viewed as enjoying God's favour, even though he was a descendant of Ham and an ancestor of Babylon and Assyria.

The genealogies have their saints and sinners, too. We hear of the unrestrained violence of Lamech (4:23–24), but also of Enoch, who 'walked with God' (5:24). Another important detail hidden in these family trees concerns the birth of Noah, since we are told that his father, Lamech, 'named him Noah, saying, "Out of the ground that the Lord has cursed this one shall bring us relief from our work and from the toil of our hands."' (5:29). This is not how we often frame the story of Noah, but it seems significant in terms of how he is introduced and clearly picks up on ideas that are important within Genesis 1—11 more widely. Can you see the connection? The 'ground' (*'adamah*) and humanity's relationship to it is a central theme in chapters 2—3 and is significant, too, in the story of Cain. The curse of the ground, or from the ground, applies in both of those stories, while work and toil are further important concerns expressed in these initial chapters of Genesis. We need to be prepared, then, to see the flood as in some sense alleviating the effects of this curse.

A striking aspect of the genealogies is the astounding lifespans of the individuals named, with Methuselah being attributed with reaching the age of nine hundred and sixty-nine. Perhaps you have your own thoughts as to how this might be explained? For example, maybe the inhabitants of the earth were thought to have enjoyed a more vibrant existence in this early period, before their days were restricted (as in 6:3). Possibly the immense lifespans are a way of indicating that humanity lived for inestimably long on the earth before we can begin to document their history or generations in a standard way. In this case, the early chapters of Genesis indicate the passing of immeasurable centuries in the lives of its 'generations'.

Chapter 10 is often described as the 'table of nations', since it concerns 'the families of Noah's sons, according to their genealogies, in their nations; and from these the nations spread abroad on the earth after the flood' (10:32). Since Noah's family is understood as the only one to survive the flood, all the populations of the earth are regarded as having descended from his sons. This is made clear in 9:19, which states, 'These three were the sons of Noah; and from these the whole earth was peopled.' The 'generations' listed in this chapter, therefore, should not just be read as a simple family tree but as an attempt to catalogue all the nations known by name at the time of writing and to represent their relation to each other in terms of kinship. However, the table of nations also indicates the fulfilment of the blessing to be fruitful and multiply and fill the earth. Although there are hints that some of the spreading of the populations occurred after the time described (for example, v. 5, 'From these the coastland peoples spread'; v. 18, 'Afterward the families of the Canaanites spread abroad'), there is no suggestion that this might have involved the emergence of further ethnic groups.

We can identify some of the peoples and places mentioned here quite easily and others are unknown. What is clear is that Noah's sons are understood as the 'fathers' of different groups of peoples and correspond broadly to three distinct regions. Japheth's descendants belong to the north and west, chiefly Asia Minor (Turkey) and Armenia, and a little further round the Mediterranean, including Cyprus (Elishah and Kittim) and Rhodes (Rodanim) (see 10:4). Tarshish is an emblematically distant place, possibly as far away as Spain. Japheth's descendants also include 'Madai', which is thought to be Media (as in 'the Medes and Persians', originally in north-western Iran).

The sons of Ham are the southern nations – Egypt and its neighbours, Ethiopia, Libya and Arabia. Egypt at times dominated Palestine, and the same can be said of two other Hamitic nations, Assyria and Babylon, while a further descendant, Caphtor (Crete), is the place from which the Philistines were understood to have originated. Rather surprisingly, Canaan is listed here as well. This people group was the closest to the Israelites, since both shared a common language (or closely related dialects) and the same geographical space. Many scholars think of Israel as effectively a Canaanite people among others – even if in its surviving traditions it wished to keep itself distinct from its neighbours. The writers of this genealogy seem keen to emphasise their ancestral distance from the Canaanites, even if their apparently unwelcome proximity was in many other respects unavoidable. It seems, then, that Ham's sons include the peoples with whom Israel and Judah often had less than friendly relations.

Shem is the ancestor of the 'Semitic' peoples, found around the Fertile Crescent. The genealogy includes, besides Eber (10:21), the presumed ancestor of the Hebrews, other nations that spoke languages that are cognate to Hebrew, such as Aram (Syria) and (more distantly) Assyria. Rather confusingly, Asshur (Assyria) is mentioned both here and as one of the sons of Ham. Both Ham and Shem are also seen as the ancestors of some Arabian cities, and two of them, Sheba and Havilah, even appear as descendants of both. Logically, we can understand how Arabia is both 'Semitic' and also far away and to the south, which could bring it into Ham's orbit. It is typical of Genesis, instead of plumping for one solution or another, to leave the options open and record both traditions.

The sons of God and the daughters of men (6:1–4)

This passage comes across as odd and difficult to understand. However, it helps if we recognise that God, as a great heavenly king and the supreme divine being, was believed to have a wider retinue of heavenly attendants, the 'sons of God'. He couldn't be expected to sit up in heaven all on his own! They weren't necessarily literally understood as 'sons' of God, since 'son' can be used to indicate the group someone belongs to. For example, the 'sons of the prophets' who are mentioned in connection with Elijah and Elisha are a 'company of prophets' rather than necessarily literally children of prophets (though some of them, at least, might have been that too). By analogy, these 'sons of God' are what we might term the 'company of heaven'.

References to the divine council, a sort of heavenly court, appear in various places in the Old Testament, such as 1 Kings 22:19–23 and Job 1:6; 2:1. Psalm 82 hints at a belief that other gods genuinely existed but had responsibilities delegated to them by the God of Israel, even if they didn't carry them out very well. Deuteronomy 32:8 (depending on which translation you're using) even suggests that each of the nations (of which there were thought to be 70) is apportioned to one of the 'sons of God'. This is especially interesting from a historical point of view, as the Canaanite high god El was supposed to have 70 sons.

Did you spot hints of the existence of a plurality of heavenly beings in Genesis 1 and 3? In Genesis 1:26, God says, 'Let *us* make humankind in *our* image, according to *our* likeness.' However, the next verse then continues in the singular:

So God created humankind in his image,
  in the image of God he created them;
  male and female he created them.

In other words, the 'us' of the company of heaven (if that's what it is) isn't incompatible with seeing God himself as the creator, any more than it is wrong to say Christopher Wren built St Paul's Cathedral, when we know perfectly well that it was the work of many other people too, even if the design was his. The text can comfortably flip back and forth between the two.

In Genesis 3:22, God says, 'See, the man has become like *one of us*, knowing good and evil.' Once again, the assumption seems to be that God isn't the only divine being. Perhaps you might have noticed other motifs that are common to chapters 3 and 6? One is the blurring of the boundary of human and divine (here by intermarriage with the sons of God, rather than by grasping at divine qualities such as 'knowledge of good and evil' and immortality). The other is human mortality as a consequence and limitation. The couple were expelled from the garden, lest they 'take also from the tree of life, and eat, and live for ever' and here in 6:3, their days are limited to 120 years.

There are echoes of chapter 3, too, in the heavenly beings' desire for the women: 'they saw that they were fair' (literally, 'they saw that they were good'), just like the woman 'saw that the tree was good for food, and that it was a delight to the eyes' in 3:6. I think we can assume the women weren't necessarily morally good, but good-looking, or good to have, like the fruit. Desire and transgression seem to be coming into the narrative yet again. Genesis 6:1–4 shows the flip side of the idea that humans shouldn't try to gain divine qualities by emphasising that divine beings shouldn't transgress on to the human level either. This strange story lies at the root of the idea in 1 Corinthians 11:10 that women should keep their heads covered 'because of the angels'. It's wise to wear a hat in case some miscreant divine being looks down and is attracted to you!

However, it is not explicitly spelled out that these relationships are prohibited rather than just belonging to the distant imagined past. In fact, 6:1–4 can be read, at least in part, as a story of origins. You might be wondering who the 'Nephilim' are. Well, it might be that the readers of Genesis were asking the same question – or at least that they wanted to know how the Nephilim originated. These people are mentioned again in Numbers 13:33, where they appear to be giants. The men who spied out the promised land describe seeing Nephilim there and as feeling like grasshoppers by comparison. The story in Genesis 6:1–4 may therefore set out to explain how these intimidating people could have come into being. In fact, the idea that the original inhabitants of Canaan were especially tall crops up again several times (see Deuteronomy 2:10, 20–21; 3:11; Amos 2:9).

Like chapters 1—3, though, this little story may also help to explain the place of humans in the world. Here it's a question of humans' relation to the wider divine realm rather than to God, other earthly life or each other. Have a look at Psalm 8, which explores similar themes to 1:26-28, including human domination of nature and awe before God. In wondering that the God who established the heavens should bestow humanity with his care, the psalmist exclaims, 'Yet you have made them [humankind] a little lower than God [or the divine beings]' (Psalm 8:5). It's astonishing that the human and divine should be placed in such close hierarchy at all. Do you think Genesis 6 is nonetheless insisting that there is a definite line between them that should not be crossed?

The flood: sin, flood, sacrifice, blessing and covenant (6:5—9:17)

Sin

In case we haven't had enough sin so far, it seems to peak before the flood. According to 6:5, 'the wickedness of humankind was great in the earth, and… every inclination of the thoughts of their hearts was only evil continually.' Did you notice the recurrence of the word 'humankind' (or 'humanity') here? It's the same word, *'adam*, that we see in chapters 2—3. God regrets the creation of humanity and, in his grief, resolves to blot them out 'from the ground' (note that other keyword, *'adamah*, 'ground', again). The echoes between the stories of the garden of Eden and the flood suggests that we shouldn't just read chapter 3 on its own as the story of 'the fall'. Instead, it belongs as part of a string of 'fallings' by humanity that causes the cursing of (or from) the ground, thereby making their existence harder.

We saw earlier that there are two creation stories. There appear to be duplicate versions of the flood story, too, but in this case they are interwoven together. This is most obvious in connection with the number of animals going into the ark. Try comparing 6:19-20 with 7:2-3. The 'two by two' version we all know seems to have the last say, though. Look at 7:8-9, 14-15, which directly contradict 7:2-3! You will see that the differences in content go hand-in-hand with alternative names for God – either 'God' or 'the Lord' – and this helps us identify the two traditions at work in the rest of the story, even where they fit more smoothly together. In fact, you might have noticed that 'God' and 'the Lord' are used in blocks throughout Genesis 1—11, and this may reflect two underlying traditions. Did you see that the first creation story refers only to 'God' and the second speaks instead of 'the Lord God'? Scholars think that the Eden story may originally have just used 'the Lord' like much of the rest of Genesis 1—11, but that the combination 'Lord God' was used to ensure readers would recognise that he was the same 'God' as referred to in chapter 1.

Right at the beginning of the flood story, we have alternative accounts of the sin that prompts God to 'blot out' what he had made. The first, as we've just seen, concerns humanity's wickedness which causes them to be wiped out 'from the ground' (*'adamah*), but the second, in 6:11–13, instead refers to 'the earth' (*'erets*) and 'all flesh' and not 'humans' or 'the ground' at all. In fact, 6:11–13 mentions the 'earth' six times in these three verses! The earth is 'corrupt', 'ruined' or even 'destroyed', because 'all flesh had corrupted [ruined/destroyed] its ways upon the earth'. ('Corrupt', 'ruin' and 'destroy' are all ways of translating the same Hebrew verb.) It's a matter of 'boomerang' justice: what 'all flesh' has done will be done to it in return. It has corrupted/destroyed/ruined its ways, destroying/ruining the earth, and therefore God will send a flood of water to 'destroy them along with the earth'.

Here, then, corruption is something of which 'all flesh' is guilty. But what is 'all flesh'? You might imagine it refers to human beings: after all, we don't expect animals to sin. But, surprisingly, the phrase must include non-human life as well as human, since we soon hear that 'all flesh in which is the breath of life' will be destroyed in the flood: 'everything that is on the earth shall die' (6:17; see also 7:21). Look through the story of the flood and you'll see that 'all flesh' is referred to repeatedly: two 'of every living thing, of all flesh' are brought into the ark (6:19, 7:15–16), and 'every living thing that is with you of all flesh' comes out at the end (8:17), while God's promise never again to destroy also relates to 'all flesh' (9:11, 15–17). So 'all flesh' means all living things, and God resolves to 'destroy them' not just '*from* the ground', as in 6:7, but '*along with* the earth' (6:13). The scale of the destruction, and of the guilt, is therefore magnified as compared with 6:5–7. It's no longer about humanity's sin and destruction 'from the ground', but wholescale corruption, including 'all flesh' and the 'earth' itself.

The flood

There are also differences in the description of the flood. It's worth reading the story carefully to see if you can spot any repetitions or inconsistencies. Did you notice how, in one version of the flood found in 7:4, it is simply said to rain for 40 days and nights? A much more graphic picture is presented in 7:11, which describes how 'all the fountains of the great deep burst forth, and the windows of the heavens were opened'. The thought here is that there is water above the firmament (the 'dome' of heaven) that might be let down through the 'windows of heaven', but that there is also water stored under the earth. This is released through the 'fountains of the deep', which feed the seas and springs from beneath. The picture seems to be of water invading the earth from above and below in a very dramatic way, and many people read this as symbolising the reversal of creation. All living things, apart from those preserved on the ark, are washed away, reversing the work of days five and six of creation. The boundary between sea and dry land blurs as water engulfs the earth, and even the separation of the waters above and below the earth appears to be reversed as water pours in from both directions.

Here, an underlying idea is that order and blessing in creation do not exist apart from ethical behaviour. Different spheres of order are interdependent, and ethical disorder has an impact on the rest of creation and requires divine intervention. Do you remember how, in chapters 3—4, the curses related to the ground or an individual's relation to the ground? Now in the flood story, a similar principle is at work, but the disaster is cosmic in its scope, affecting (and perhaps dismantling) all of creation. You might notice, though, that there are some aspects of creation that are not 'undone'. For example, is there any mention of darkness or plants? You might expect this if the writer is trying to show that God is fully reversing his creative work. What we seem to have, then, is a partial collapse triggered by corruption, and then God's redemptive intervention to cleanse the earth, preserve life and reinstate the created order.

This event is also described in Genesis as a 'flood' (or 'flood of water') which is 'on the earth' (6:17; 7:6–7, 10, 17; 9:11, 15, 28). It is easy to think that we know what is meant by this, but you have to remember that we're only reading Genesis in an English translation. The Hebrew word translated here as 'flood' isn't one we meet in other places where normal flooding, such as from excess rainfall or overflowing rivers, occurs. In fact, we only find it in one other place outside Genesis, in Psalm 29:10, where the Lord is said to sit enthroned over 'the flood'. There the idea seems to be that he sits as king above the waters of heaven. If so, Genesis describes the descent of the massive heavenly water reserves on to the earth. This, then, is a cosmic catastrophe, a one-off event, not just 40 days of rain.

But, of course, although the flood was intended to 'blot out' everything on the earth because of its corruption and violence, not quite everyone and everything was guilty. Noah, we are told, was 'righteous' and 'blameless'. He 'walked with God' (6:9) and so 'found favour in the sight of the Lord' (6:8). I'm sure you remember the story of Noah taking all the animals into the ark, with his family and 'every kind of food that is eaten'. Have you noticed, though, how much God directs everything he does? Once Noah, his family and the animals are aboard, it is even God who shuts them in. All other living things are blotted out, yet God remembers Noah and all the animals that are in the ark, and he causes the waters to subside.

Another well-known part of the flood story is the sending out of the birds. Ancient navigators used to take birds with them in their vessels simply because their flight path could indicate the direction of land, even when it was beyond the horizon. Here, though, the ark is stuck on the top of a mountain, so the experiment is to see whether there is any dry land that might support life. After the dove brings back an olive leaf, Noah is reassured that the earth is drying, so after waiting another week, he removes the covering of the ark and they disembark.

Sacrifice

Did you know that when Apollo 11's lunar module landed on the moon in July 1969, Buzz Aldrin celebrated Communion before they opened the door and stepped on to the surface for the first time? He said afterwards, 'I could think of no better way to acknowledge the Apollo 11 experience than by giving thanks to God.' Perhaps it's not surprising to see Noah doing something similar after his miraculous escape and safe arrival back on to a drying earth. He builds an altar and offers a sacrifice (or rather, multiple sacrifices – one of every clean animal and bird) to the Lord. And the Lord in his turn resolves:

I will never again curse the ground ['adamah] because of humankind ['adam], for the inclination of the human ['adam] heart is evil from youth; nor will I ever again destroy every living creature as I have done.
GENESIS 8:21

This is striking in a number of ways. First, the theme of the ground being cursed because of humanity is pretty familiar by now. Do you remember Genesis 3:17, when the ground is cursed 'because of you' (addressed to 'the human' who had eaten the forbidden fruit)? Then Cain is 'cursed from the ground' which had received his brother's blood in 4:11. Less familiar is the prophecy at Noah's birth in 5:29, which promises relief from the ground that the Lord has cursed. It seems that now, after the flood, we may be getting to that point.

But the other notable thing is God's accommodation to human sin. He will never again curse the ground because of humankind, because the 'inclination of the human heart is evil from youth'. These evil inclinations are no longer narrated as specific to certain individuals or events, but sin is now recognised to be part of the human condition. Can you think where else in Genesis 1—11 we see a concession offered after punishment? It's quite a consistent theme.

Blessing

As well as not cursing, God also blesses. When Noah and all the living things with him come out of the ark, God commands him to bring them out 'so that they may abound [or swarm] on the earth, and be fruitful and multiply on the earth' (8:17). Does this remind you of anything? The same phrase is used in chapter 1, where it is most immediately applied to the creatures of the sea (1:22) and to human beings (1:28). As the fish and humans are the first and last of the living things to be made, we should assume that the blessing of procreation is also intended for the birds and land animals (who are made in-between), but 8:17 seems to confirm this quite directly. Given that these are the sole survivors of the flood, fruitfulness is doubtless seen as necessary for such a depleted population. Nevertheless, the echo of chapter 1 may also suggest a fresh start for creation.

In 9:1 and 9:7, the blessing of fruitfulness is specifically repeated to Noah and his children. These blessings frame a passage that concerns human relations with animals and food, and the implications of humanity being made in God's image. This section takes us back to Genesis 1:26–30, but (as we'll see) with modifications in the light of all that has passed in-between.

Just as the resolve not to curse is overshadowed by the acknowledgement of human evil, even the blessing has a darker side. Do you remember that when food is gifted in 1:29–30, both humans and animals are given plants to eat? Now in chapter 9, meat-eating is mentioned for the first time and the relation between humans and animals is characterised by 'fear' and 'dread'. This seems to be quite far removed from the potential companionship considered in 2:19–20. It marks a change in relationship, with animals now being subject to human aggression. Possibly the 'violence' in the earth that was identified before the flood is still played out here. Now all living things are to experience this fear, and they are said to be 'given' into 'your hand' (9:2). This idea is then repeated with the statement, 'I give you everything', and is explained further in the declaration that 'every moving thing that lives shall be food for you'.

The idea that 'everything' could eaten might strike you as odd in the Old Testament, where, of course, there were strict dietary laws. However, this particular passage seems to assume that the law had not yet been given, so at this time there was no distinction between clean and unclean animals. In fact, we see two perspectives on this in the first chapters of Genesis, one being reflected in pairs of animals going into the ark without differentiation between species, and the other in the statement that there were seven pairs of each clean animal and only one pair of unclean.

An important aspect of the permission to eat meat is that it is limited. The animal's life is perceived to be in its blood, so the blood must never be consumed, but rather should be drained out first. This sounds strange, but it is a way of recognising the sanctity of life: eating meat involves the death of a creature and this must be taken seriously and dealt with respectfully. (There is more about this in Leviticus 17:10–14 and Deuteronomy 12:20–25.) The killing of humans is utterly prohibited, either by their fellow humans or by other animals, the reason for this being that God made them in his own image. It is reassuring to hear the idea of the image being unconditionally affirmed, despite all that has transpired.

Covenant

Genesis 8:21–22 shows the Lord promising never again to curse the ground, but to provide an unceasing rhythm of day and night, summer and winter, as long as the earth endures. After the ensuing blessings, we have a promise, the first covenant in the Old Testament (9:8–17). Usually a covenant is a two-way agreement, with promises and undertakings on both sides. Here, though, God freely makes a solemn undertaking with nothing specific required in return. If you read the passage carefully, you will also see that this undertaking is made towards all living things who came out of the ark, 'all flesh'. It guarantees that he will never again send the flood to destroy all flesh or the earth, and the sign of this is the rainbow, which is understood as God's bow, which is set in the clouds. This may partly be an explanatory story for the rainbow, but it is also understood as God's own *aide memoire* not to destroy the earth in this way again.

Understanding the flood story

The biblical flood story has very ancient roots, going back to texts from Babylonia and Assyria, the earliest of which may be dated hundreds of years before the formation of the people of Israel. However, despite striking similarities with these flood stories, the one in Genesis is also distinctive in certain respects. These differences merit attention because we can see that here the narrators have decided to disagree with earlier versions and to tell the story differently.

Probably the most obvious difference is that in the other ancient Near Eastern versions of the story, one God causes the flood and another rescues the flood hero. This, in many ways, is much easier to understand than God doing apparently quite contradictory things. In fact, this isn't just an ancient problem. If you look at modern pictures of the flood, you will find some in which it is represented as a terrible scene of judgement, with helpless people drowning, and you'll see others with the happy inhabitants of the ark enjoying their salvation, often with the rainbow already visible in anticipation of God's promise. Holding together judgement and salvation is difficult, and when you think about it, it is quite an extraordinary thing to attempt when the older versions of the story were so much easier. However, in a monotheistic faith, the idea that everything comes from one God is fundamental.

Tied in with monotheism, though, is the idea that God is just and therefore addresses wickedness, but that he also ultimately cares for creation and seeks its preservation. In Genesis, the corruption of the earth was intolerable and could not be ignored, whereas in the Atrahasis epic the motivation for the flood is that humanity was becoming too numerous and noisy and disturbing the gods' peace. Now, it might be that 'noise' is actually about becoming too powerful, and that the gods are understood as somehow having felt threatened by this: it's not necessarily quite as trivial as we might at first suppose. Nonetheless, we can see immediately that Genesis offers a very different account of why the flood came about. Having the same God providing salvation at the same time as destruction also says something very deep about the necessity of dealing with sin and about God's commitment to the earth, even when he deems it necessary to remove nearly everything on it. We see here a double departure from Genesis' antecedents, since not only is the reason for judgement very different, but God pointedly and repeatedly blesses his creatures with fruitfulness after the flood.

However, Genesis also drops certain things from the story. For a start, the hero – here Noah, rather than Atrahasis or Utnapishtim – is not granted eternal life after the flood. In fact, in the next instalment he makes the very human error of becoming drunk! Keeping the boundaries between the human and divine firmly set is consistent with the rest of Genesis 1–11, but it is also a consequence of monotheism. In fact, in ancient Egyptian and Greek traditions, wine was discovered by the gods, but this passage brings it back down to earth.

The other difference, which we might miss, is that in Genesis God expresses no compassion or regret for those who are destroyed. In the Babylonian and Assyrian stories, of course, the god who shows compassion is the one who effects some kind of rescue through the ark, rather than the engineer of the catastrophe. In Genesis, God's decision is viewed as the correct one, and he has already taken mitigating action by directing Noah to build the boat in which the seeds of all subsequent life will be preserved. As a result, there is no suggestion that he might regret the loss of life that he effected, except insofar as he resolves never to destroy everything again.

Noah's drunkenness and the cursing of Ham (9:18–27)

This is a rather unpleasant story, with anti-Canaanite sentiment only thinly veiled here. Did you notice how the fact that 'Ham was the father of Canaan' is highlighted just before, in 9:18? Canaan is mentioned again in verses 25–27, as suffering for the trespass of his father, Ham. It is highly ironic that a story that gave us the root (through the name 'Shem') for our term 'anti-Semitism' itself lays the foundation for other forms of racial discrimination, albeit aimed to affirm Semitic superiority and the suppression of Canaan. This passage has been used to justify apartheid in South Africa and black slavery, since the descendants of Ham include Africans. The tale also offends modern sensibilities about guilt and punishment. If

Noah lay naked in his tent, then surely that Ham saw him is more the father's fault than the son's? And why should Ham's son be cursed instead of Ham himself?

Quite why Ham was seen as guilty is a matter of debate, but it seems that besides the fault of seeing his father's nakedness, he should have sought to help him rather than simply informing his brothers. (Look at Isaiah 51:17–18 for the idea that sons should help a drunken parent.) As for the cursing of Canaan, the rationale for this is opaque, but for the fact that the writers had more motivation for creating and preserving a story which spoke of Canaan in this way than they would of Ham. However, it is possible that there was an alternative version of the story in which Canaan was brother to Shem and Japheth. He is referred to as their 'brother' in 9:25, and in the previous verse, it is said that it was Noah's youngest son who had seen him, even though Ham is always mentioned as the second of three brothers.

The passage seems to relate to the occupation of the land by the people of Israel and by the descendants of Japheth. No one is entirely sure why Japheth is mentioned together with Shem here. One suggestion is that the reference is to the Philistines, since Japheth is seen as the ancestor of the inhabitants of the Mediterranean and the Philistines are said to have come from Kittim (Cyprus), one of Japheth's descendants, in Numbers 24:24. However, according to Genesis 10:14, the Philistines are descended from Ham. It is also surprising to hear of the Philistines being blessed, if this is what is intended here.

The idea that the inhabitants of the land became the Israelites' slaves appears in Joshua 9, Judges 1:28, 30, 33 and 1 Kings 9:20–21. However, these references obviously sit alongside other accounts that suggest that the Canaanites were cast out of the land or slaughtered, or that the two groups lived alongside each other. The passage seems, then, to serve to justify or explain the subjugation of the Canaanites and perhaps offers hope that their subordination will be achieved.

It is important to acknowledge that, although the Bible can be a tremendous motivator for good and for deep ethical concern, religious texts can also have a potentially dangerous character. This is one such passage, where the human side of such writing is alarmingly apparent. However, did you notice who it was that uttered the curse? Often the less salutary sentiments expressed in the Old Testament are attributed to human beings rather than to God. The other curses of Genesis 1—11 are introduced in God's voice, often with an explanation of why they have occurred: try comparing 3:14 and 17.

The story of the cursing of Canaan has an explanatory function for the authors' time, but how this happened is told, not condoned. Can you see how God's name does not appear in this passage, except in being called upon to bless Shem and Japheth? (Actually, the Hebrew reads 'Blessed be the Lord, the God of Shem,' but this doesn't make much sense in the context of a blessing of the brothers, so most translations assume a small correction here.) Noah curses, but God is called upon to bless.

A subsidiary aspect of the story is that it functions to tell of the origins of winemaking. We notice again that Noah is described as a 'man of the soil/ground' (*'adamah*). Perhaps this is another way in which he fulfils his father's words: 'Out of the ground that the Lord has cursed this one shall bring us relief from our work and from the toil of our hands' (Genesis 5:29). The cheering effects of wine are mentioned in Psalm 104:15 and Judges 9:13, but it was also a way of drowning the sorrows of those in distress and poverty: have a look at Proverbs 31:6–7.

The Tower of Babel (11:1–9)

Genesis 10 tells how the peoples of the earth evolved by descent from Noah's sons and how the 'nations spread abroad on the earth after the flood' (10:32). It seeks to explain how the different nationalities arose and how they are related to each other, but also shows the fulfilment of the call to be fruitful and multiply and fill the earth. The increased population forms a backdrop to chapter 11, at the beginning of which, we are told, 'the whole earth had one language and the same words'. The story is no longer concerned with just one family, but with humanity as a whole.

Strictly speaking, chapters 10 and 11 don't run together perfectly. Chapter 10 mentions different languages (look at 10:5, 20, 31) and the dispersal of different populations over the earth. But at the beginning of chapter 11, although people had had migrated from the east (or perhaps 'eastwards' – the meaning of the Hebrew isn't very clear), the picture seems to be of everyone having settled in the land of Shinar (Babylonia: see 10:10), where they had built a city. To read it as a coherent thread, we need to think of chapter 10 as concerning a very extended period, and chapter 11 as being located somewhere near the beginning of this time.

The offence committed in this story is that the people resolve to build a tower 'with its top in the heavens', and to make a name for themselves. Once again, humanity is seeking to overreach itself. If humans can't gain immortality or wisdom, and if they shouldn't intermingle with the 'sons of God', the next assault on the divine is to try to build up into heaven!

You may have read about 'high places', places of worship in the Old Testament that were usually prohibited because they represented places of worship other than the temple. Jerusalem is often described as a 'holy mountain' (even though it wasn't actually very high), and Moses goes up Mount Sinai to meet with God and receive the tablets of the law. Even the story of the transfiguration, when Jesus's appearance changed and his clothes became dazzlingly white so that the disciples saw something of his divinity, happened on a mountain. The idea of heaven as 'up' is a common thread.

Temples or other locations of special contact with the divine might be thought of as places where heaven and earth meet. For example, after Jacob had his dream of a ladder going up to heaven, he named the place 'Bethel', which means 'house of God': it was somewhere where heaven and earth intersect.

These concepts are reflected, too, in the famous Mesopotamian 'temple towers' or ziggurats, which were structures comprising successively receding levels, rather like a wedding cake. They most probably had a shrine, thought to be the dwelling place of the god, at the top. In fact, a notable ziggurat, in Babylon itself, was called Etemenanki, 'temple of the foundation of heaven and earth', and is reputed to have been seven stories tall. Another interesting connection between the building activities in this story and the ziggurat in Babylon is the form of construction – with bricks and bitumen instead of stone and mortar.

Can you think of where you might have read about God 'coming down' to see what was happening on earth or to meet with people? The same phrase occurs in relation to God meeting Moses on Mount Sinai (Exodus 19:11, 18, 20; 34:5) or coming down to the tent of meeting (Numbers 11:25; 12:5). However, the sense of God personally engaging with human affairs on earth is already there in Genesis 3:8, when God walks in the garden in the breeze, and his conversation with Cain suggests a similar kind of interaction. In each case, it happens in a place where heaven and earth meet – if not on Sinai or in the tent of meeting, then after a sacrifice has been offered (in chapter 4) or in the garden of Eden (in chapter 3), elsewhere known as the 'garden of God' (Ezekiel 28:13) or 'holy mountain of God' (Ezekiel 28:14, 16).

Have you noticed any further echoes of previous strands of Genesis 1—11 here? For a start, the city and tower had been built by humankind (*'adam*, 11:5). God's concerns are expressed as a dialogue again: 'Come, let us go down, and confuse their language there' (11:7). This might remind you of other situations where the divide between human and divine is in danger of being breached. Do you remember 3:22–23, just before the human couple are evicted from the garden? 'The Lord God said, "See, the man has become like one of us, knowing good and evil; and now, he might reach out his hand and take also from the tree of life, and eat, and live forever" – therefore the Lord God sent him forth from the garden of Eden.'

This resonates with Babel in several ways. First, God talks in the plural to the company of heavenly beings; second, he can see where human aspirations are heading and the threat they may pose in the future; and third, he takes pre-emptive action by evicting or scattering them. Of course, even creating humanity required particular thought and again concerned a potential link between the human and divine: 'Let us make humankind [*'adam*] in our image, according to our likeness' (1:26). You might think God's concerns in chapter 11 are rather prescient for our own times: 'This is only the beginning of what they will do; nothing that they propose to do will now be impossible for them' (11:6). Of course, what we can do and understand is limited, but nonetheless, we are not always able to apply the brakes helpfully ourselves! As you read back through the passage, look out for echoes with other stories from Genesis 1—11, but also ask yourself whether you can identify any implications of relevance for today.

The city where this coordinated human enterprise took place has traditionally been referred to as 'Babel'. This is rather odd, as everywhere else in the Old Testament (except in Genesis 10:10) exactly the same place name is translated as 'Babylon'. This is the city state that was at the centre of the Babylonian empire, under whose oppression Jerusalem fell in 586BC. However, the rather irregular translation (strictly, a transliteration rather than a translation) does fit rather nicely with the etymology of the place name: it was called 'Babel' because there the Lord made a 'babble' of their languages (the Hebrew word is *balal*).

Despite what we might think, the reference to Babylon doesn't really help with dating the story. While it might be intended as an indictment of the hated empire, this is far from certain. The story might have arisen many hundreds of years earlier to explain why Babylon (or its ziggurat) was at that time incomplete. (Apparently it was begun under Nebuchadnezzar I in the twelfth century BC but wasn't finished for many hundreds of years.) Alternatively, it could have been intended to critique Solomon's building enterprises or other developments at a different time. Possibly the story also enjoys challenging Babylon's folk etymology as the 'gate of God' (*bab-ilim*) and offering an alternative explanation of its name and relation to the divine. You might like to think about which explanation you find most plausible.

As the story stands, it provides an account of how different languages might have developed, but of course it also anticipates the election of Abram. Prior to this point, God is seen as relating to all of humanity, or in the case of the flood story, selecting one righteous person to save while the rest were wiped out. Now the families of the earth are dispersed across the known world and speak different languages, the solution will be to elect one man, though we soon discover that the intention is that through him all the families of

Tips for reading Genesis 1—11 and what to look for

the earth will be blessed (or bless themselves). In fact, a bridge is made to the Abram story already at the end of chapter 11, where the family tree ends with Abram and the childless Sarai settling in Haran.

8

Genesis 1—11 in the Bible

As we have seen, Genesis 1—11 provides a backdrop affirming God's commitment to the whole world. It reveals him as the creator of all living things and of the wider cosmos as viewed from the perspective of the earth, while showing his concern for all of humanity rather than solely for one people. Most of the rest of the Bible will indeed focus on that people, but nonetheless, this wider context and hope shines through in various places.

Indeed, reading Genesis 1—11 in the light of the Bible as a whole invites this wider perspective to be assumed from Genesis onwards as well as to be read backwards from the New Testament. Hope for all the world to know the Lord and to call on him in one language, a 'pure speech', is expressed in Zephaniah 3:9. Links are also made with the day of Pentecost, when, according to Acts 2, everyone assembled could hear the apostles speaking as if in their own tongue. No direct allusion is made to the Babel story in Acts itself, but it is widely understood as a reversal of the confusion of languages and as offering an inclusive picture of representatives of many different nations hearing the good news in Jerusalem.

However, the New Testament does not just relate back to Babel and creation. We saw how the *'adam*, the human, was Everyman, a 'type' or model of flawed humanity. Christ is understood in the New Testament as a second 'Adam', a new 'type' of human. Through him is offered the forgiveness of sin (e.g., Matthew 1:21; 26.28; Acts 5:31; 10:43; 13:38–39; Romans 6:11; Colossians 1:14; Revelation 1:5), but also the end of the limitations besetting human existence as elaborated in Genesis 3: mourning, crying, pain and death (Revelation 21:4).

Genesis firmly insists on the barriers between the human and divine: the mortality and earthliness of humans, and their eviction from the garden and God's presence there. By contrast, Revelation looks forward to the end of death, but also to the dissolution of the barriers between God and creation, in the form of a new heaven and earth coming down out of heaven (Revelation 21:1, 5) and God dwelling in the new Jerusalem (Revelation 21:3, 22–23; 22:3–4). The Bible begins with creation and with humanity dwelling in God's presence in Eden, but it ends as it began, with creation renewed and restored to God's presence.

9

Questions for reflection or discussion

1 What kind of stories do you think Genesis 1—11 contains?

2 What message do you take from them?

3 What has surprised you about Genesis 1—11?

4 How would you encourage others to read these chapters?

5 What would the Bible be missing without Genesis 1—11?

6 Has Genesis 1—11 challenged you in any way?

7 How does Genesis 1—11 help you understand the proper relationship between God and humanity, and between human beings and other creatures?

8 How might Genesis 1—11 motivate ecological concerns?

9 How do you understand being made 'in the image of God'? How might it affect how you live your life or relate to others?

10 In what ways do you see human life as caught between being made in the image of God, and yet formed of the dust of the ground and subject to sin?

11 Are there any 'Towers of Babel' today – situations where humans try to overreach their limits improperly? How might we know?

12 How might Genesis 1—11 shape your faith?

BRF

Transforming
lives and communities

Christian growth and understanding of the Bible

Resourcing individuals, groups and leaders in churches for their own spiritual journey and for their ministry

Church outreach in the local community

Offering two programmes that churches are embracing to great effect as they seek to engage with their local communities and transform lives

Teaching Christianity in primary schools

Working with children and teachers to explore Christianity creatively and confidently

Children's and family ministry

Working with churches and families to explore Christianity creatively and bring the Bible alive

parenting for faith

Visit **brf.org.uk** for more information on BRF's work

brf.org.uk

The Bible Reading Fellowship (BRF) is a Registered Charity (No. 233280)